The COURAGE Scripture Reference Guide

by
Edwin Louis Cole

A Division of Harrison House, Inc.
Tulsa, Oklahoma

Unless otherwise indicated, all Scripture quotations are taken from the *King James Version* of the Bible.

The Courage Scripture Reference Guide
ISBN 0-89274-400-6
Copyright © 1986 by Edwin Louis Cole
Edwin Louis Cole Ministries
International Headquarters
P. O. Box 626
Corona del Mar, CA 92625

Southwest Offices
P. O. Box 610588
Dallas, TX 75261

Published by Honor Books
A Division of Harrison House, Inc.
P. O. Box 35035
Tulsa, Oklahoma 74153

Printed in the United States of America. All rights reserved under International Copyright Law. Contents and/or cover may not be reproduced in whole or in part in any form without the express written consent of the Publisher.

CONTENTS

1 "Despise Not Thy Youth"	7
2 Courage	17
3 WIMPS: Made in America	27
4 Sex	35
5 How Do You Spell "Release"?	43
6 The Invisible Man	49
7 Working Hard, Going Nowhere	61
8 Bend, Bow or Burn	71
9 Write It On Your Shorts	83
10 CHAMPIONS: Men Who Never Quit	93

COURAGE
Outline and Reference Guide

Chapter 1 — "DESPISE NOT THY YOUTH"
I. Making the most of youth
  A. Don't waste your youth.
     Titus 2:6 TLB
     In the same way, urge the young men to behave carefully, taking life seriously.
  B. Recognize that despite your youth you are still a man.
     Jeremiah 1:6-8 TLB
     "O Lord God," I said, "I can't do that! I'm far too young! I'm only a youth!"
     "Don't say that," he replied, "for you will go wherever I send you and speak whatever I tell you to. And don't be afraid of the people, for I, the Lord, will be with you and see you through."
  C. Remember that God works through young men.
     Examples:
     1. Joseph — Genesis 37:1-11
     2. David — 1 Samuel 17:11-35
     3. Daniel — Daniel 1-3
     4. Jesus — Luke 2:41-49
  D. Recognize that there are advantages to being young.
     1. Strength
        Proverbs 20:29 TLB
        The glory of young men is their strength...

2. Ability to learn quickly

   1 John 2:13 TLB

   ...And I am writing to you younger boys...because you, too, have learned to know God our Father.

3. Ready molding of character

   Lamentations 3:27

   It is good for a man that he bear the yoke in his youth.

E. Never be ashamed of your youth.

   1 Timothy 4:12 TLB

   Don't let anyone think little of you because you are young...

   1. Acknowledge your youth, turn it to God, and revel in it.

      Ecclesiastes 11:9 TLB

      Young man, it's wonderful to be young! Enjoy every minute of it! Do all you want to; take in everything, but realize that you must account to God for everything you do.

   2. Realize and capitalize on the advantages of your youth.

      Proverbs 19:20 TLB

      Get all the advice you can and be wise the rest of your life.

II. .Destructive forces facing youth today

   A. The "Me Generation" philosophy which breeds anarchy and rebellion

      2 Timothy 3:1-4 TLB

      You may as well know this too, Timothy, that in the last days it is going to be very difficult to be a Christian.

For people will love only themselves and their money; they will be proud and boastful, sneering at God, disobedient to their parents, ungrateful to them, and thoroughly bad.

They will be hardheaded and never give in to others; they will be constant liars and troublemakers and will think nothing of immorality. They will be rough and cruel, and sneer at those who try to be good.

They will betray their friends; they will be hotheaded, puffed up with pride, and prefer good times to worshiping God.

B. False doctrine

1 Timothy 4:1 TLB

But the Holy Spirit tells us clearly that in the last times some in the church will turn away from Christ and become eager followers of teachers with devil-inspired ideas.

C. The anti-hero syndrome

Proverbs 17:15 TLB

The Lord despises those who say that bad is good, and good is bad.

D. Weakening of the father role model

2 Timothy 3:2 TLB

...they will be...disobedient to their parents, ungrateful to them...

E. Weakness in some church leadership

1. Pastors who are a "lid" instead of a covering

Jeremiah 6:13,14 TLB

...Yes, even my prophets and priests! You can't heal a wound by saying it's not there! Yet the priests and prophets give assurances of peace when all is war.

2. Placating and pleasure-seeking youth pastors

   Isaiah 56:10-12 TLB

   For the leaders of my people—the Lord's watchmen, his shepherds—are all blind to every danger. They are featherbrained and give no warning when danger comes. They love to lie there, love to sleep, to dream.

   And they are as greedy as dogs, never satisfied; they are stupid shepherds who only look after their own interest...

   "Come," they say. "We'll...have a party;...This is really living; let it go on and on, and tomorrow will be better yet!"

3. Elders who create cynicism and give undue criticism to young people

   Ezekiel 34:4,5 TLB

   "You haven't taken care of the weak nor tended the sick nor bound up the broken bones nor gone looking for those who have wandered away and are lost. Instead you have ruled them with force and cruelty.

   "So they were scattered, without a shepherd. They have become a prey to every animal that comes along."

III. God's pattern for the Church

   A. Prophets emphasize the specific Word God has given them.

   Amos 3:8

   The lion hath roared, who will not fear? the Lord God hath spoken, who can but prophesy?

   B. Pastors balance the truth of the prophet with the total life of the congregation.

1 Peter 5:1,2 TLB

And now, a word to you elders of the church...Fellow elders, this is my plea to you: Feed the flock of God; care for it willingly...

C. Youth pastors give young men the meat of the Word of God, and discipline them.

1 Timothy 4:11,13 TLB

Teach those things and make sure everyone learns them well...read and explain the Scriptures to the church; preach God's Word.

D. The characteristics of the kingdom (church) emanate from the character of the king (pastor).

Hosea 4:9 TLB

And thus it is: "Like priests, like people"—because the priests are wicked, the people are too...

E. A pastor who loves truth will produce a congregation that loves truth.

1 Thessalonians 1:6,7 TLB

So you became our followers and the Lord's...Then you yourselves became an example to all the other Christians in Greece.

IV. Paul-Timothy discipleship

A. Senior pastors and old men should take time to disciple young associates and younger men.

Psalm 71:18 TLB

And now that I am old and gray, don't forsake me. Give me time to tell this generation (and their children too) about all your mighty miracles.

B. Older men should not yield to the Saul syndrome.

1 Samuel 18:8 TLB

Of course Saul was very angry. "What's this?" he said to himself. "They credit David with ten thousands and me with only thousands. Next they'll be making him their king!"

C. Young associates and younger men should receive the benefits of the older men's experience.

Proverbs 15:5,14 TLB
Only a fool despises his father's advice; a wise son considers each suggestion...

A wise man is hungry for the truth, while the mocker feeds on trash.

Proverbs 1:8,9 TLB

Only fools refuse to be taught. Listen to your father and mother. What you learn from them will stand you in good stead; it will gain you many honors.

D. Young men should avoid the Absalom syndrome—that is, taking advantage of their position to undermine their senior's authority.

2 Samuel 15:1-6 TLB

Absalom...got up early every morning and went out to the gate of the city; and when anyone came to bring a case to the king for trial, Absalom called him over and expressed interest in his problem.

He would say, "...I surely wish I were the judge; then anyone with a lawsuit could come to me, and I would give him justice!"...

So in this way Absalom stole the hearts of all the people of Israel.

V. God's patterns and principles

A. God has given us power to overcome any obstacle, enemy or attack through the truth of the patterns and principles in His Word.

Jeremiah 23:29

Is not my word like as a fire? saith the Lord; and like a hammer that breaketh the rock in pieces?

Luke 1:37 ASV

For no word from God shall be void of power.

B. It is God's desire for His Church to know His patterns and principles.

Deuteronomy 29:29

The secret things belong unto the Lord our God: but those things which are revealed belong unto us and to our children for ever, that we may do all the words of this law.

C. As disciples, it is our right to know the truth.

John 8:31,32

...If ye continue in my word, then are ye my disciples indeed;

And ye shall know the truth, and the truth shall make you free.

VI. The pattern of the parable of the prodigal

A. *Rebellion*: Sin never cares about anything except gratifying its own desires, heedless of the consequences.

Luke 15:12

And the younger of them said to his father, Father, give me the portion of the goods that falleth to me...

B. *Ruin*: The prodigal began his ruin with the words, "Give me."

Luke 15:13,14

...the younger son gathered all together, and took his journey into a far country, and there wasted his substance with riotous living.

And when he had spent all, there arose a mighty famine in that land; and he began to be in want.

Chapter 1

    C. *Repentance*: The pivotal point between ruin and reconciliation is characterized by the words, "Make me."

    Luke 15:17-19

    And when he came to himself, he said,... I will arise and go to my father, and will say unto him, Father, I have sinned against heaven, and before thee,

    And am no more worthy to be called thy son: make me as one of thy hired servants.

    D. *Reconciliation*: The prodigal returns home to his father.

    Luke 15:20

    And he arose, and came to his father. But when he was yet a great way off, his father saw him, and had compassion, and ran, and fell on his neck, and kissed him.

    E. *Restoration*: The father accepts the son and restores him to his rightful position.

    Luke 15:22-24
    But the father said to his servants, Bring forth the best robe, and put it on him; and put a ring on his hand, and shoes on his feet:...

    For this my son was dead, and is alive again; he was lost, and is found...

    F. *Recommitment*: Words of confession and contrition reveal an attitude of repentance and obedience.

    Psalm 51:3,4,10,12 TLB

    For I admit my shameful deed...You saw it all, and your sentence against me is just...

    Create in me a new, clean heart, O God, filled with clean thoughts and right desires...*make me* willing to obey you.

1. The words "make me" show submission to authority, a willingness to change, acceptance of personal responsibility—the beginning of real manhood.

2. Are you ready to speak these words and to become a real man?

QUESTIONS TO CONSIDER:

1. Read 1 Timothy 4:12 in which Paul exhorts Timothy to let no one despise his youth. Study the second part of the verse. What could Timothy do to keep others from despising his youth?

2. Chapter One lists some conditions which can hinder young men from reaching their full potential as champions for God. What are some hindrances you are experiencing?

What can you do to overcome them?

3. What are the steps of the pattern of the Prodigal Son?

This parable illustrates the high cost of low living. What does rebellion cost us?

What does reconciliation and restoration cost us?

What did it cost God? (See Rom. 5:10.)

SCRIPTURE TO MEMORIZE:

Psalm 119:9

Chapter 2 — COURAGE

I. Need of courage

    A. It takes courage to face reality.

    Psalm 51:6

    Behold, thou desirest truth in the inward parts...

    B. It takes courage to admit fault.

    Proverbs 28:13 TLB

    A man who refuses to admit his mistakes can never be successful...

    C. It takes courage to change. (Example.: King Asa.)

    2 Chronicles 15:8

    And when Asa heard these words, and the prophecy of Obed the prophet, he took courage, and put away the abominable idols out of all the land...and renewed the altar of the Lord...

    D. It takes courage to make decisions.

    Joshua 24:15
    ...choose you this day whom ye will serve;...but as for me and my house, we will serve the Lord.

    E. It takes courage to hold convictions.

    Acts 4:18-20

    And they called them, and commanded them not to speak at all nor teach in the name of Jesus,

    But Peter and John answered and said...Whether it be right in the sight of God to hearken unto you more than unto God, judge ye.

    For we cannot but speak the things which we have seen and heard.

    F. It takes courage to resist peer pressure and to dare to be different.

Psalm 119:51,52 TLB

Proud men hold me in contempt for obedience to God, but I stand unmoved. From my earliest youth I have tried to obey you; your Word has been my comfort.

(Also **Dan. 1:8.**)

G. It takes courage to submit to righteousness.

Psalm 119:30 TLB

....help me...to obey your laws, for I have chosen to do right.

H. It takes courage to say "no."

Psalm 119:101

I have refrained my feet from every evil way, that I might keep thy word.

I. It takes courage to admit a desire to be a man of God.

Psalm 119:115

Depart from me, ye evildoers: for I will keep the commandments of my God.

Hebrews 11:25

Choosing rather to suffer affliction with the people of God, than to enjoy the pleasures of sin for a season.

II. Prerequisites of courage

A. Courage must be directed by knowledge. You must know right from wrong in order to know what to resist and what to yield to.

Psalm 119:104

Through thy precepts I get understanding: therefore I hate every false way.

B. It takes courage to stand your ground; courage coupled with wisdom to know when to run.

Psalm 16:8

I have set the Lord always before me: because he is at my right hand, I shall not be moved.

1 Timothy 6:11 TLB

Oh, Timothy, you are God's man. Run from all these evil things and work instead at what is right and good...

(Also **Gen. 39:12.**)

C. Courage can be the virtue of the wise or the vanity of fools.

Proverbs 14:16 TLB

A wise man is cautious and avoids danger; a fool plunges ahead with great confidence.

III. Expressions of courage

A. Moral courage enables a person to encounter hatred, disapproval and contempt without departing from what is right.

Psalm 119:157

Many are my persecutors and mine enemies; yet do I not decline from thy testimonies.

B. The Bible is a book of moral courage. It contains many examples of men of courage:

1. John the Baptist — Matthew 14:3-10

2. Daniel — Daniel 6

3. David — 1 Samuel 17

4. Paul — Acts 27; 28:1-5

5. Stephen — Acts 7

6. Gideon — Judges 6,7

Chapter 2

Hebrews 12:1 TLB

Since we have such a huge crowd of men of faith watching us from the grandstands, let us strip off anything that slows us down or holds us back...and let us run with patience the particular race that God has set before us.

C. Boldness is a form of courage.

Hebrews 13:6

So that we may boldly say, The Lord is my helper, and I will not fear what man shall do unto me.

1. If you keep quiet before ungodly men, you give them the advantage.

Proverbs 10:10 TLB
Winking at sin leads to sorrow; bold reproof leads to peace.

1 Peter 3:15

...and be ready always to give an answer to every man that asketh you a reason of the hope that is in you...

2. Successful men are bold in their identification with their belief, product or activity, and in their confession of it.

Psalm 119:46

I will speak of thy testimonies also before kings, and will not be ashamed.

Romans 1:16

For I am not ashamed of the gospel of Christ: for it is the power of God unto salvation to every one that believeth...

3. If we are willing to overcome our fear of men, openly identify with Jesus, and be bold in our confession of Him, we will become overcomers.

Matthew 10:28,32,33

And fear not them which kill the body, but are not able to kill the soul: but rather fear him which is able to destroy both soul and body in hell...

Whosoever therefore shall confess me before men, him will I confess also before my Father which is in heaven.

But whosoever shall deny me before men, him will I also deny before my Father which is in heaven.

Revelation 12:11

And they overcame him (the devil) by the blood of the Lamb, and by the word of their testimony; and they loved not their lives unto the death.

4. When we lose our life in identification with Jesus Christ, we find a greater life we would never have known otherwise.

Matthew 10:39 AMP

Whoever finds his [lower] life will lose [the higher life], and whoever loses his [lower] life on My account will find [the higher life].

IV. Hindrances to courage

  A. Moral cowardice

    1. Moral cowardice causes men to shrink from duty and danger, to dread pain, and to yield to fear.

1 Samuel 15:24 TLB

"I have sinned," Saul finally admitted. "Yes, I have disobeyed your instructions and the command of the Lord, for I was afraid of the people and did what they demanded."

    2. The fear of man is a form of moral cowardice.

Chapter 2

Proverbs 29:25

The fear of man bringeth a snare...

3. Moral cowardice is the ruin of manhood.

   Numbers 13:33

   And there we saw the giants,...and we were in our own sight as grasshoppers, and so we were in their sight.

B. Double-mindedness

1. The double-minded waver between right and wrong because they are undecided.

   1 Kings 18:21 TLB

   Then Elijah talked to them. "How long are you going to waver between two opinions?"...

2. They profess to hate sin, but have a lingering love for it.

   James 4:1 TLB

   What is causing the quarrels and fights among you? Isn't it because there is a whole army of evil desires within you?

3. They do not have a right understanding of good and evil.

   Hebrews 5:14

   But strong meat belongeth to them that are of full age, even those who by reason of use have their senses exercised to discern both good and evil.

C. Associations with the insincere "churchwise."

1. The churchwise show no courage.

   Proverbs 28:1

   The wicked flee when no man pursueth: but the righteous are bold as a lion.

2. They are playing religious games. Their deception is dangerous to your dedication.

   2 Timothy 3:5 TLB

   They will go to church, yes, but they won't really believe anything they hear. Don't be taken in by people like that.

V. Choice of courage

   A. Life is composed of your choices and constructed by your words.

   Deuteronomy 30:19 TLB

   "...today I have set before you life and death, blessing or curse. Oh, that you would choose life; that you and your children might live!"

   Proverbs 18:21

   Death and life are in the power of the tongue...

   B. Don't be embarrassed about your commitment to God.

   Mark 8:38 TLB

   "And anyone who is ashamed of me and my message in these days of unbelief and sin, I, the Messiah, will be ashamed of him when I return in the glory of my Father, with the holy angels."

   C. Be bold in word and deed.

   Acts 4:13

   Now when they saw the boldness of Peter and John, and perceived that they were unlearned and ignorant men, they marvelled; and they took knowledge of them, that they had been with Jesus.

   D. Learn to discern between good and evil, the truth and a lie.

Chapter 2

1 Kings 3:9

Give therefore thy servant an understanding heart...that I may discern between good and bad...

E. Don't be moved by every person's personality, persuasion and belief.

Ephesians 4:14

That we henceforth be no more children, tossed to and fro, and carried about with every wind of doctrine, by the sleight of men, and cunning craftiness, whereby they lie in wait to deceive.

F. Don't listen to teaching which contradicts what you know is right.

Proverbs 19:27 TLB

Stop listening to teaching that contradicts what you know is right.

G. Find a godly pastor who can help you and be your example in word, lifestyle, love, spirit, faith, purity.

Philippians 3:17,18 TLB

Dear brothers, pattern your lives after mine and notice who else lives up to my example. For I have told you often before, and I say it again now with tears in my eyes, there are many who walk along the Christian road who are really enemies of the cross of Christ.

H. Judge yourself by your actions, not by your intentions.

Proverbs 21:8 TLB

A man is known by his actions. An evil man lives an evil life; a good man lives a godly life.

I. Lay a right foundation for your character.

2 Corinthians 7:1 TLB

Having such great promises as these, dear friends, let us turn away from everything wrong, whether of body

Courage

    or spirit, and purify ourselves, living in the wholesome fear of God, giving ourselves to him alone.

J. Remember: The choice is yours, the glory is God's.

2 Peter 3:18

But grow in grace, and in the knowledge of our Lord and Saviour Jesus Christ. To him be glory both now and for ever. Amen.

QUESTIONS TO CONSIDER:

1. Read Joshua 1:6-9 in which the Lord gives Joshua instructions for leading the children of Israel into the Promised Land. Why did God tell Joshua he needed courage?

Why was freedom from fear a possibility for Joshua?

2. Now study Acts 4:13,31. Remember, only a few weeks before this occasion, these same men had deserted Jesus and fled in terror. What factors do you believe accounted for their change from cowardice to boldness? (See also Acts 1:8.)

Are these factors present in your life?

3. Now look at 2 Timothy 1:6-8. Is fear an emotion, or a spirit which affects the emotions?

Where do you think fear comes from?

According to this passage, what qualities of spirit does God give us?

Look again at verse 8. If you had a spirit of fear, what might your attitude be toward an uncompromising testimony of Christ, and toward those who are boldly proclaiming such a testimony?

What is the response of Jesus Christ to those who allow themselves to be embarrassed by the Gospel? (See Matt. 11:6 and Mark 8:38.)

SCRIPTURES TO MEMORIZE:

Deuteronomy 31:6; 2 Timothy 1:7; Romans 1:16

Chapter 3 — WIMPS: MADE IN AMERICA

I. Determine to follow after success and godliness.

Deuteronomy 8:18 TLB

"Always remember that it is the Lord your God who gives you power to become rich..."

A. Don't kill your ego — sanctify it. Purify your motives and use your ego to achieve great things for God.

Mark 12:30

And thou shalt love the Lord thy God with all thy heart, and with all thy soul, and with all thy mind, and with all thy strength...

B. Concentrate on your strengths, not your weaknesses.

Romans 12:6 TLB

God has given each of us the ability to do certain things well...

C. Recognize your gifts, talents, and abilities and dedicate them to God.

Romans 12:1 TLB

And so, dear brothers, I plead with you to give your bodies to God. Let them be a living sacrifice, holy — the kind he can accept...

1. Let God put creative ideas in your mind and godly desires in your heart.

Psalm 37:4 TLB

Be delighted with the Lord. Then he will give you all your heart's desires.

2. Let Him fulfill His will by enabling you to realize those dreams.

Chapter 3

Psalm 37:5 TLB

Commit everything you do to the Lord. Trust him to help you do it and he will.

D. Recognize that as a man you were created by God to be successful — a hero and a champion.

Genesis 1:26 TLB

Then God said, "Let us make a man — someone like ourselves, to be the master of all life upon the earth and in the skies and in the seas."

II. Beware of religion — the enemy of spiritual fulfillment.

Matthew 15:6

...Thus have ye made the commandment of God of none effect by your tradition.

A. Religion is the devil's counterfeit of Christianity. It is one of the tools Satan uses to destroy men and usurp their rightful position.

John 10:10 TLB

"The thief's purpose is to steal, kill and destroy..."

B. Religion leads to the bondage of failure, poverty and mediocrity.

Galatians 4:9 TLB

And now that you have found God...how can it be that you want to go back again and become slaves once more to another poor, weak, useless religion...?

C. Religion teaches that it is a sin to achieve great things; it preaches humility but practices inferiority.

Colossians 2:8 TLB

Don't let others spoil your faith and joy with their philosophies, their wrong and shallow answers built

on men's thoughts and ideas, instead of on what Christ has said.

D. Religion causes men to bury their gifts, talents and abilities in an effort to achieve spirituality.

Matthew 25:25

And I was afraid, and went and hid thy talent in the earth: lo, there thou hast that is thine.

E. Religion perpetuates error; men who build their lives on it will never fulfill the God-inspired goals for their lives.

Psalm 127:1

Except the Lord build the house, they labour in vain that build it...

III. Learn to identify wimps.

A. Wimps: Men who are products of a substitute society.

Titus 1:16 TLB

Such persons claim they know God, but from seeing the way they act, one knows they don't...

1. They substitute manners and culture for the power of God's presence.

1 Corinthians 4:20 TLB

The kingdom of God is not just talking; it is living by God's power.

2. They substitute status symbols for the fruit of the Spirit.

Colossians 3:2,3 TLB

Let heaven fill your thoughts; don't spend your time worrying about things down here. You should have as little desire for this world as a dead person does...

(Also **Matt. 13:22**.)

Chapter 3

    3. They substitute fantasy for reality.

       Romans 1:25 TLB

       Instead of believing what they knew was the truth about God, they deliberately chose to believe lies...

       (Also Jer. 23,24.)

    4. They substitute respectability for righteousness.

       John 12:43

       For they loved the praise of men more than the praise of God.

       John 5:44 TLB

       "No wonder you can't believe! For you gladly honor each other, but you don't care about the honor that comes from the only God!"

    5. They substitute works for faith.

       Hebrews 11:6

       But without faith it is impossible to please him...

    6. They substitute softness for gentleness. (God is forbearing, but not soft.)

       Romans 2:4,5

       Or despisest thou the riches of his goodness and forbearance and longsuffering; not knowing that the goodness of God leadeth thee to repentance?

B. Wimps: Men who are soft.

       Hebrews 12:4

       Ye have not yet resisted unto blood, striving against sin.

    1. Soft men can't take rough times. They make truces and compromises with the flesh, the world and the devil.

1 Corinthians 10:13 TLB

But remember this — the wrong desires that come into your life aren't anything new and different. Many others have faced exactly the same problems before you. And no temptation is irresistible. You can trust God to keep the temptation from becoming so strong that you can't stand up against it...

2. Jesus was gentle but not soft. He taught a ruthlessness required by God.

Mark 9:43,44 TLB

"If your hand does wrong, cut it off. Better live forever with one hand than be thrown into the unquenchable fires of hell with two!"

3. Soft men don't have more because they settle for less. (Example: The children of Israel.)

Joshua 18:3

And Joshua said unto the children of Israel, How long are ye slack to go to possess the land, which the Lord God of your fathers hath given you?

4. Soft men forfeit victory by seeking to avoid pain.

1 Corinthians 9:25 TLB

To win the contest you must deny yourselves many things that would keep you from doing your best...

IV. Don't be a wimp!

1 Corinthians 16:13 TLB

Keep your eyes open for spiritual danger; stand true to the Lord; act like men; be strong.

A. Don't compromise with sin. Fight until you have victory. Then you can live in peace.

Ephesians 6:13 TLB

So use every piece of God's armor to resist the enemy whenever he attacks, and when it is all over, you will still be standing up.

B. Develop your own relationship with God.

John 14:17

Even the Spirit of truth; whom the world cannot receive, because it seeth him not, neither knoweth him: but ye know him: for he dwelleth with you, and shall be in you.

1. You are never too young to hear from God. Hearing from God doesn't depend on age, but on relationship.

   John 10:27

   My sheep hear my voice, and I know them, and they follow me.

2. If you don't seek God's counsel, you may be deceived into making a truce with the enemy. (Example: Joshua and the Gibeonites.)

   Joshua 9:14,15

   And the men took of their victuals, and asked not counsel at the mouth of the Lord. And Joshua made peace with them, and made a league with them, to let them live: and the princes of the congregation sware unto them.

C. Crucify the flesh, but live a resurrected life.

Romans 6:5

For if we have been planted together in the likeness of his death, we shall be also in the likeness of his resurrection.

1. Die to pride, fear and the vain things of the world and the flesh.

   Romans 6:6

   Knowing this, that our old man is crucified with him, that the body of sin might be destroyed, that henceforth we should not serve sin.

2. But live for God-given dreams, divinely-inspired desires which are realized through the resurrection power within you.

> **Philippians 2:12,13**
>
> ...work out your own salvation with fear and trembling. For it is God which worketh in you both to will and to do of his good pleasure.

3. Determine to live up to the potential that is within you, placed there by God.

> **Philippians 3:12 TLB**
>
> I don't mean to say I am perfect. I haven't learned all I should even yet, but I keep working toward that day when I will finally be all that Christ saved me for and wants me to be.

   a. Depend upon God to promote you.

> **Psalm 75:6,7 TLB**
>
> For promotion and power come from nowhere on earth, but only from God. He promotes one and deposes another.

   b. Trust that your gift will make a way for you.

> **Proverbs 22:29 NIV**
>
> Do you see a man skilled in his work? He will serve before kings; he will not serve before obscure men.

QUESTIONS TO CONSIDER:

1. "God didn't call men to be trucemakers, but peacemakers. And peace comes through victory." In the Old Testament God instructed His people to deal ruthlessly with their enemies and have no pity on them. Why? (Read Deut. 7:16,25,26, Num. 33:55, and Josh. 23:11-13.)

2. Now read 1 Samuel 15:1-28. What were God's instructions to Saul?

Chapter 3

Saul was a man who could not bring himself to be ruthless with his enemies, the Amalekites. He wanted to preserve a portion — that which he considered attractive and desirable. What was the immediate consequence of Saul's disobedience?

3. The Bible teaches that if we do not destroy our enemy, our enemy will destroy us. In 2 Samuel 1:1-10 we have the pitiful account of Saul's death. Who ultimately destroyed Saul?

4. In 1 Corinthians 10:11 the Apostle Paul says that these Old Testament accounts were recorded as object lessons for us. When God tells us to deal ruthlessly with something in our lives, He always has a good reason. Do you have habits, acquaintances or a lifestyle which God has instructed you to cut off?

Do you believe compromise in these areas could be costly?

SCRIPTURE TO MEMORIZE:

1 Corinthians 10:13

Chapter 4 — SEX

I. Sex: God's gift

   A. God made everything good, including sex.

Genesis 1:31
And God saw everything he made, and, behold, it was very good...

     1. God made sex as a means of replenishing the earth.

Genesis 1:28

And God blessed them, and God said unto them, Be fruitful, and multiply, and replenish the earth...

     2. God made sexual energy the power that holds the family together.

Genesis 2:24

Therefore shall a man leave his father and his mother, and shall cleave unto his wife...

     3. Sex is a physical union which symbolizes the spiritual union of man and woman.

Genesis 2:24

...and they shall be one flesh.

     4. God created sex so a man and woman in the union of marriage could give themselves unreservedly to each other.

1 Corinthians 7:4 TLB

For a girl who marries no longer has full right to her own body, for her husband then has rights to it, too; and in the same way the husband no longer has full right to his own body, for it belongs also to his wife.

Chapter 4

    B. God's prohibition on sex outside marriage was given to protect sex.

        Hebrews 13:4

        Marriage is honourable in all, and the bed undefiled...

        1. The woman should be the glory of the man, not the object of his lust and thus the cause of his separation from God.

           1 Corinthians 11:7 TLB

           God's glory is man made in his image, and man's glory is the woman.

        2. God's Word is filled with warnings to young men concerning their unbridled passions.

           Proverbs 7:24,25 TLB

           Listen to me, young men, and not only listen but obey; don't let your desires get out of hand...

           1 Corinthians 6:18

           Flee fornication...he that committeth fornication sinneth against his own body.

II. Programming the conscience

    A. God's Word washes the mind and programs the conscience to righteousness.

        Ephesians 5:25,26

        ...Christ also loved the church, and gave himself for it;

        That he might sanctify and cleanse it with the washing of water by the word.

        Psalm 119:9 TLB

        How can a young man stay pure? By reading your Word and following its rules.

    B. The first symptom of error is taking scriptures and making them conform to one's own lifestyle.

2 Timothy 4:3,4 TLB

For there is going to come a time when people won't listen to the truth, but will go around looking for teachers who will tell them what they want to hear. They won't listen to what the Bible says but will blithely follow their own misguided ideas.

C. Perversion of life leads to perversion of the scriptures.

Romans 1:24,25 TLB

So God let them go ahead into every sort of sex sin, and do whatever they wanted to — yes, vile and sinful things with each other's bodies. Instead of believing what they knew was the truth about God, they deliberately chose to believe lies...

D. God never gave His Word so people could take it to justify their own lifestyles.

Deuteronomy 12:32 TLB

"Obey all the commandments I give you. Do not add to or subtract from them."

E. God's Word is the source of faith and the sole rule of conduct.

Matthew 4:4

...Man shall not live by bread alone, but by every word that proceedeth out of the mouth of God.

Psalm 119:112

I have inclined mine heart to perform thy statutes alway, even unto the end.

F. God's power is released to the degree that obedience is exercised.

Revelation 2:26

And he that overcometh, and keepeth my works unto the end, to him will I give power over the nations.

Chapter 4

    G. God's love is unconditional but His promises are conditional.

        Isaiah 1:19

        If ye be willing and obedient, ye shall eat the good of the land.

    H. The Holy Spirit is given to restrain the Christian so he is kept pure before God in thought, word and deed.

        Ezekiel 36:27

        And I will put my spirit within you, and cause you to walk in my statutes, and ye shall keep my judgments, and do them.

III. Sin's deception

    A. Sin always promises to please and serve, but in reality it always enslaves and dominates.

        John 8:34

        Jesus answered them, Verily, verily, I say unto you, Whosoever committeth sin is the servant of sin.

        2 Peter 2:19 TLB

        ...But these very teachers who offer this "freedom" from law are themselves slaves to sin and destruction. For a man is a slave to whatever controls him.

    B. Sin alters behavior.

        Genesis 3:6-8

        ...when the woman saw that the tree was good for food...she took of the fruit thereof, and did eat, and gave also to her husband...and he did eat.

        And the eyes of them both were opened, and they knew that they were naked; and they sewed fig leaves together, and made themselves aprons.

Sex

And they heard the voice of the Lord God walking in the garden....and Adam and his wife hid themselves from the presence of the Lord God...

C. Pornography is an example of sexual deception.

1. A person cannot engage in pornography without being affected by the unclean spirits which produced it.

Proverbs 6:27,28 TLB

Can a man hold fire against his chest and not be burned? Can he walk on hot coals and not blister his feet?

2. Pornography becomes an idolatrous activity. The image is created in the mind of the viewer.

Ezekiel 8:12

...Son of man, hast thou seen what the ancients of the house of Israel do in the dark, every man in the chambers of his imagery? for they say, The Lord seeth us not...

3. In turn pornography creates a stronghold in the mind and a snare to the life.

Psalm 106:36

And they served their idols: which were a snare unto them.

4. Idolatrous fantasizing and private sex sins are a sin against one's own manhood.

Deuteronomy 7:26

Neither shall thou bring an abomination into thine house, lest thou be a cursed thing like it...

IV. Submitting to God's yoke

Matthew 11:28,29 TLB

"Come to me and I will give you rest — all of you who work so hard beneath a heavy yoke.

Chapter 4

"Wear my yoke — for it fits perfectly — and let me teach you; for I am gentle and humble, and you shall find rest for your souls; for I give you only light burdens."

A. Knowing that you do not have sin in your life gives you an easy feeling.

Romans 8:2 TLB

For the power of the life-giving Spirit — and this power is mine through Christ Jesus — has freed me from the vicious circle of sin and death.

B. You are light-hearted when you're not burdened with guilt.

Psalm 32:5 TLB

...I finally admitted all my sins to you and stopped trying to hide them. I said to myself, "I will confess them to the Lord." And you forgave me! All my guilt is gone.

C. Being yoked to righteousness is a joy forever.

Romans 6:18

Being then made free from sin, ye became the servants of righteousness.

D. Freedom from sin allows God's glory and power to flow through your life.

1 John 3:21,22 TLB

But, dearly loved friends, if our consciences are clear, we can come to the Lord with perfect assurance and trust, and get whatever we ask for because we are obeying him and doing the things that please him.

E. To remain free from sin, program your conscience to righteousness by the Word of God.

Colossians 3:16

Let the word of Christ dwell in you richly in all wisdom...

1. Love God's Word.

    Psalm 119:97

    O how I love thy law! it is my meditation all the day.

2. Apply it to your life.

    John 13:17

    If ye know these things, happy are ye if ye do them.

QUESTIONS TO CONSIDER:

1. Numbers chapter 22 records the account of an unscrupulous prophet named Balaam who was hired by King Balak, the enemy of Israel, to pronounce curses on God's people. It was impossible for Balaam to curse those whom God had decided to bless (Num. 23:11,12), but he conceived another plan calculated to bring defeat upon the nation of Israel. He counseled Balak to tempt the people of God into sex sins — fornication and idolatry. (Num. 31:16.)

Do you believe temptation into sexual sin is still a tactic the enemy uses to bring destruction to God's people? (See Rev. 2:14.)

2. Numbers 25:9 tells us that 24,000 people perished in the plague which struck Israel as a result of their sex sins. What are some of the plagues sexual promiscuity brings to the Church and to our society today?

3. Study (in *The Living Bible*, if possible) Psalm 119:9 and 2 Timothy 2:22 in which Paul admonishes us to **flee also youthful lusts...** By contrast, what activites do these verses instruct us to pursue?

How do you think our choice of friends affects our ability to flee youthful lusts?

SCRIPTURE TO MEMORIZE:

2 Timothy 2:22

Chapter 5 — HOW DO YOU SPELL "RELEASE"?

I. The principle of release (John 20:22,23.)

   A. The principle of release states that only after sins are released are people free to become what God wants them to be.

   Matthew 6:14,15 TLB

   "Your heavenly Father will forgive you if you forgive those who sin against you; but if you refuse to forgive them, he will not forgive you."

   B. Healing takes place when, by faith, the principle of release is acted upon.

   Hebrews 12:1 TLB

   ...let us strip off anything that slows us down or holds us back, and especially those sins that wrap themselves so tightly around our feet and trip us up; and let us run with patience the particular race that God has set before us.

   C. In order to activate this principle in your own life, you should admit the Holy Spirit into your heart, and be guided and directed by Him.

   John 20:21,22 AMP

   Then Jesus...breathed on [them], and said to them, Receive (admit) the Holy Spirit!

   D. Remember: The sins you forgive are released, and the sins you do not forgive are retained in your life. If you forgive, you release; if you don't forgive, you retain.

   John 20:23 AMP

   [Now, having received the Holy Spirit and being led and directed by Him] if you forgive the sins of any one they are forgiven; if you retain the sins of any one, they are retained.

Chapter 5

II. The doorway to maturity

   A. Maturity doesn't come with age; it comes with acceptance of responsibility.

      Acts 13:22 TLB

      "...God said, 'David (son of Jesse) is a man after my own heart, for he will obey me.' "

   B. We cannot mature if we go through life blaming circumstances, or other people for our shortcomings.

      Proverbs 16:2 TLB

      We can always "prove" we are right, but is the Lord convinced?

      Proverbs 21:2 TLB

      We can justify our every deed but God looks at our motives.

      (Also **Gen. 3:11,12**.)

   C. We alone are responsible for our own life.

      2 Corinthians 5:10 TLB

      For we must all stand before Christ to be judged and have our lives laid bare — before him. Each of us will receive whatever he deserves for the good or bad things he has done in his earthly body.

III. The importance of the father/son relationship

   A. The Word of God talks about fathers and sons in various ways.

      1. **It is a wonderful heritage to have an honest father** (Prov. 20:7 TLB).

      2. **...A child's glory is his father** (Prov. 17:6 TLB).

      3. **Reverence for God gives a man deep strength; his children have a place of refuge and security** (Prov. 14:26 TLB).

B. Fathers have a God-given responsibility to their offspring.

1. Fathers are blessed when they raise their children in the fear and admonition of the Lord.

   Deuteronomy 11:18-21 TLB

   "So keep these commandments carefully in mind...Teach them to your children. Talk about them when you are sitting at home, when you are out walking, at bedtime, and before breakfast!...so that...you and your children will enjoy the good life awaiting you..."

2. Fathers are cursed if they neglect their family responsibility.

   Proverbs 17:25 TLB

   A rebellious son is a grief to his father and a bitter blow to his mother.

C. Sons also have responsibilities toward their fathers.

1. They are to honor their fathers.

   Ephesians 6:2,3 TLB

   Honor your father and mother. This is the first of God's Ten Commandments that ends with a promise. And this is the promise: that if you honor your father and mother, yours will be a long life, full of blessing.

   Proverbs 20:20 TLB

   God puts out the light of the man who curses his father or mother.

2. They are to submit to their father's authority in the Lord.

   Colossians 3:20 TLB

   You children must always obey your fathers and mothers, for that pleases the Lord.

3. They are not to allow their father's sins to ruin their life.

Hebrews 12:15 TLB

...Watch out that no bitterness takes root among you, for as it springs up it causes deep trouble, hurting many in their spiritual lives.

4. They are to make sure their heart is clean before God concerning their father, forgiving him of his sins, offenses and neglect.

Ephesians 4:31,32 TLB

Stop being mean, bad-tempered and angry. Quarreling, harsh words, and dislike of others should have no place in your lives.

Instead, be kind to each other, tender-hearted, forgiving one another, just as God has forgiven you because you belong to Christ.

IV. The Nature of Life

  A. There are only two things you do in life: Enter and leave.

    1. How you leave determines how you enter.

Galatians 6:7

Be not deceived; God is not mocked: for whatsoever a man soweth, that shall he also reap.

    2. How you leave one sphere or experience of life will determine how you enter the next.

2 Peter 1:10,11 TLB

So, dear brothers, work hard to prove that you really are among those God has called and chosen...And God will open wide the gates of heaven for you to enter into the eternal kingdom of our Lord and Savior Jesus Christ.

B. Change produces crisis in life.
  1. Crisis is normal to life.
     John 16:33
     ...In the world ye shall have tribulation...
  2. Crisis has sorrow in it, but sorrow is life's greatest teacher.
     Ecclesiastes 7:3 TLB
     Sorrow is better than laughter, for sadness has a refining influence on us.
     Psalm 119:71
     It is good for me that I have been afflicted; that I might learn thy statutes.
  3. All true joy is borne out of sorrow.
     Psalm 126:5
     They that sow in tears shall reap in joy.
     Psalm 30:5
     ...weeping may endure for a night, but joy cometh in the morning.
  4. God wants every change in the lives of His children to be good.
     Romans 8:28 TLB
     And we know that all that happens to us is working for our good if we love God and are fitting into his plans.
C. Learn to take advantage of the crises in your life.
  1. Don't let crises separate you from God. Use them to bring you closer to Him. Let God take you through each crisis to the next stage of life.
     Romans 8:38 TLB
     For I am convinced that nothing can ever separate us from...the love of God demonstrated by our Lord Jesus Christ when he died for us.

2. Always remember that God is for you, not against you.

Psalm 56:9 TLB

The very day I call for help, the tide of the battle turns. My enemies flee! This one thing I know: God is for me!

3. Be careful not to waste your youth brooding over what someone else has done to you.

Isaiah 43:14,18 TLB

The Lord, your Redeemer, the Holy One of Israel, says: ...forget all that — it is nothing compared to what I'm going to do!

QUESTIONS TO CONSIDER:

1. Read the story of Joseph in Genesis 37 and 39-45. List the crises in Joseph's life.

2. Did these crises separate Joseph from God, or bring him closer to Him?

3. Did the crises Joseph encountered make him bitter or better?

What indicates to you that Joseph had forgiven his brothers, and that God had healed him of the wounds caused by their offense? (Read also Gen. 50:15-21.)

4. List some ways God worked through Joseph's crises.

Who else benefited from Joseph's victory over crisis?

5. Are you facing, or have you recently faced, a crisis in your life? If so, after studying the life of Joseph and Chapter Five of *Courage,* do you believe God is able to make your crisis work for your good and the good of others?

What must you do in order for God to do His part?

SCRIPTURE TO MEMORIZE:

Romans 12:21

Chapter 6 — THE INVISIBLE MAN

I. Character and personality

    A. Personality is not the same as character.

    Proverbs 26:23 TLB

    Pretty words may hide a wicked heart, just as a pretty glaze covers a common clay pot.

    B. Personality is after the outward man and is temporal.

    1 Samuel 16:7 TLB

    But the Lord said to Samuel, "Don't judge by a man's face or height...I don't make decisions the way you do! Men judge by outward appearances, but I look at a man's thoughts and intentions."

    C. Character is built in private. It develops out of a lifetime of individual decisions which either enhance or diminish it.

    Psalm 119:30

    I have chosen the way of truth: thy judgments have I laid before me.

    2 Timothy 2:21

    If a man therefore purge himself from these, he shall be a vessel unto honour, and meet for the master's use, and prepared unto every good work.

II. Character and the honor of God

    A. What honors and dishonors God?

        1. Obedience to His Word honors God; disobedience dishonors Him.

Chapter 6

Proverbs 14:2 TLB

To do right honors God; to sin is to despise Him. (Also 1 Sam. 15:22,23.)

2. Faith in God honors Him; unbelief dishonors Him.

Hebrews 11:6

But without faith it is impossible to please him: for he that cometh to God must believe that he is, and that he is a rewarder of them that diligently seek him.

3. Trust in Jesus as Savior honors God; rejection of the Son dishonors the Father.

John 6:29 TLB

..."This is the will of God, that you believe in the one he has sent."

Luke 10:16

...and he that despiseth me (Jesus) despiseth him that sent me.

4. God is honored when His children refuse to succumb to temptation.

James 1:12 TLB

Happy is the man who doesn't give in and do wrong when he is tempted, for afterwards he will get as his reward the crown of life that God has promised those who love him.

B. A man who has learned to honor God privately will show good character in his decisions publicly.

Psalm 119:101,102,104

I have refrained my feet from every evil way, that I might keep thy word.

I have not departed from thy judgments: for thou hast taught me...

Through thy precepts I get understanding: therefore I hate every false way.

Examples:

1. Mordecai (Esth. 2:21,22.)
2. Shadrach, Meshach and Abednego (Dan. 3:16-18.)
3. Joseph (Gen. 39:7-12.)

C. God honors those who honor Him.

1 Samuel 2:30 TLB

"....I will honor only those who honor me, and I will despise those who despise me."

(Also Ps. 91:14,15; John 12:26.)

Examples:

1. Mordecai: He was elevated by God to the office of prime minister. (Esth. 10:3.)
2. Shadrach, Meshach and Abednego: They were promoted and prospered. (Dan. 3:30.)
3. Joseph: He became second in command to Pharaoh. (Gen. 41:39,40.)

D. When a man honors God, he strengthens his character, increases the stature of his manhood, and finds favor with God and man.

Job 17:9 TLB

"...the righteous shall move onward and forward; those with pure hearts shall become stronger and stronger."

Psalm 84:5,7 TLB

Happy are those who are strong in the Lord, who want above all else to follow your steps...They will grow constantly in strength and each of them is invited to meet with the Lord in Zion.

Proverbs 4:18 TLB

But the good man walks along in the ever-brightening light of God's favor...

(Also **Luke 2:40,52; Ps. 89:17.**)

   E. The honor of God is the criterion for the Christian way of living.

Ecclesiastes 12:13 TLB

Here is my final conclusion: fear God and obey his commandments, for this is the entire duty of man.

III. The requirement of truth

   A. All sin is deceitful in its character.

Hebrews 3:13

But exhort one another daily, while it is called To day; lest any of you be hardened through the deceitfulness of sin.

   B. The Christian must know the truth so he can recognize the lies of Satan and fight for the honor of God.

Proverbs 2:6-9 TLB

For the Lord grants wisdom! His every word is a treasure of knowledge and understanding. He grants good sense to the godly...He shows how to distinguish right from wrong, how to find the right decision every time.

     1. God's Word is the source of truth.

John 17:17 TLB

Make them pure and holy through teaching them your words of truth.

     2. God's Spirit guides into all truth.

John 16:13

Howbeit when he, the Spirit of truth, is come, he will guide you into all truth...

C. Honesty is the core of integrity.

Proverbs 11:3,5 TLB

A good man is guided by his honesty; the evil man is destroyed by his dishonesty...

The upright are directed by their honesty; the wicked shall fall beneath their load of sins.

Proverbs 12:5,13 TLB

A good man's mind is filled with honest thoughts; an evil man's mind is crammed with lies...

Lies will get any man into trouble, but honesty is its own defense.

D. God loves honesty but hates cheating.

Proverbs 11:1 TLB

The Lord hates cheating and delights in honesty.

IV. The importance of prayer

A. Prayer leads to knowledge of God.

1. Prayer requires honesty with God.

Psalm 51:6 TLB

You deserve honesty from the heart; yes, utter sincerity and truthfulness. Oh, give me this wisdom.

Psalm 145:18

The Lord is nigh unto all them that call upon him, to all that call upon him in truth.

2. True prayer is getting with God, sharing with Him the cares and needs of our life and letting Him share with us His concern for the world.

Chapter 6

Philippians 4:6 TLB

Don't worry about anything; instead, pray about everything; tell God your needs and don't forget to thank him for his answers.

Jeremiah 33:3

Call unto me, and I will answer thee, and shew thee great and mighty things, which thou knowest not.

3. It is normal to pray.

Luke 18:1

...men ought always to pray, and not to faint.

Ephesians 6:18 TLB

Pray all the time. Ask God for anything in line with the Holy Spirit's wishes...

4. Neglect of prayer will separate us from God as much as yielding to temptation.

2 Chronicles 15:2 TLB

..."The Lord will stay with you as long as you stay with him! Whenever you look for him, you will find him. But if you forsake him, he will forsake you."

B. Prayer leads to friendship with God.

1. Friendship with God is life's greatest treasure.

Psalm 25:14 TLB

Friendship with God is reserved for those who reverence him. With them alone he shares the secrets of his promises.

Proverbs 3:32 TLB

...he [God] gives his friendship to the godly.

2. Being with God dispels loneliness.

Psalm 73:25,26

Whom have I in heaven but you? And I desire no one on earth as much as you!

My health fails; my spirits droop, yet God remains! He is the strength of my heart; he is mine forever!

C. Prayer leads to power with God.

1. Men who know how to pray develop a boldness toward life that enables them to be more than conquerors.

    James 5:16,17 TLB

    ...The earnest prayer of a righteous man has great power and wonderful results.

    Elijah was as completely human as we are, and yet when he prayed earnestly that no rain would fall, none fell for the next three and one half years!

    Then he prayed again, this time that it would rain, and down it poured...

    Romans 8:31,37

    ...If God be for us, who can be against us?...

    Nay, in all these things we are more than conquerors through him that loved us.

2. Those who know how to pray know that God is for them.

    Psalm 56:9 TLB

    The very day I call for help, the tide of the battle turns. My enemies flee! This one thing I know: God is for me!

3. The result of prayer in private is a life of boldness and courage in public.

    Acts 4:31

    And when they had prayed,...they were all filled with the Holy Ghost, and they spake the word of God with boldness.

Chapter 6

4. Prayer is an invisible tool which is wielded in a visible world. (Example: The Apostle Peter.)

Acts 12:4,5,7 TLB

...Herod's intention was to deliver Peter to the Jews for execution after the Passover. But earnest prayer was going up to God from the Church for his safety all the time he was in prison.

..suddenly there was a light in the cell and an angel of the Lord stood beside Peter!...And the chains fell off his wrists!

V. The visible and the invisible

    A. The natural world is made up of the elements of the supernatural world. That which is visible is made up of that which is invisible.

    Hebrews 11:3 TLB

    By faith — by believing God — we know that the world and the stars — in fact, all things — were made at God's command; and that they were all made from things that can't be seen.

    B. Love is invisible; giving is visible.

    John 3:16

    For God so loved the world, that he gave his only begotten Son, that whosoever believeth in him should not perish, but have everlasting life.

    C. Honor is invisible; obedience is visible.

    Luke 6:46 TLB

    "So why do you call me 'Lord' when you won't obey me?"

    D. The degree of invisible love is evidenced by the degree of visible giving.

1 John 3:16

Hereby perceive we the love of God, because he laid down his life for us: and we ought to lay down our lives for the brethren.

E. The quality of love for God is also reflected in obedience.

John 14:21 TLB

"The one who obeys me is the one who loves me..."

F. Giving cannot be a substitute for obedience.

1 Samuel 15:22 TLB

..."Has the Lord as much pleasure in your burnt offerings and sacrifices as in your obedience? Obedience is far better than sacrifice. He is much more interested in your listening to him than in your offering the fat of rams to him."

Proverbs 21:27 TLB

God loathes the gifts of evil men, especially if they are trying to bribe him!

G. Honoring God results in both giving and obedience.

VI. Overcoming peer pressure

A. God deals with His children according to His Word, not accordng to society's norm.

Proverbs 16:25

There is a way that seemeth right unto a man, but the end thereof are the ways of death.

B. The man who wants to follow God's Word and live his life in purity will find acceptance with God, but not always with his peers.

Psalm 119:51,61,63,65 TLB

Proud men hold me in contempt for obedience to God, but I stand unmoved...

Chapter 6

> Evil men have tried to drag me into sin, but I am firmly anchored to your laws...
>
> Anyone is my brother who fears and trusts the Lord and obeys him...
>
> Lord, I am overflowing with your blessings, just as you promised.

C. As Christians, the honor of God should be more important to us than the honor of our peers.

John 5:44 TLB

> "No wonder you can't believe! For you gladly honor each other, but you don't care about the honor that comes from the only God!"

D. If you are a child of God, don't submit your personal character to the character of your peer group.

Exodus 23:2,3 TLB

> "Don't join mobs intent on evil. When on the witness stand, don't be swayed in your testimony by the mood of the majority present..."

E. If you make a quality decision to honor God in your thoughts, words, motives, and deeds, God will honor you.

John 12:26

> If any man serve me, let him follow me; and where I am, there shall also my servant be: if any man serve me, him will my Father honour.

QUESTIONS TO CONSIDER:

1. What is the difference between personality and character?

List some personality traits.

List some elements of character.

2. In what ways do invisible qualities become visible? (See Matt. 7:16-20; 13:34,35.)

3. The majority of our money, time and energy is spent on developing the outward man. In what ways can we develop the inner man?

Which of these two is God most concerned with?

SCRIPTURE TO MEMORIZE:

Matthew 7:16,17

Chapter 7 — WORKING HARD, GOING NOWHERE

The Ingredients of Manhood.

I. Accountability

    A. Every man has to face his accountability for his own actions.

        Romans 14:12

        So then every one of us shall give account of himself to God.

        Luke 12:48 TLB

        "...Much is required from those to whom much is given..."

    B. Desire for authority without the willingness to accept accountability for one's actions leads to a no-growth situation.

        Proverbs 28:13 TLB

        A man who refuses to admit his mistakes can never be successful. But if he confesses and forsakes them, he gets another chance.

    C. Every man is accountable for six areas of responsibility in his own life (1 Tim. 3:1-11):

    1. Reputation

        1 Thessalonians 5:22

        Abstain from all appearance of evil.

        2 Corinthians 6:3 TLB

        We try to live in such a way that no one will ever be offended or kept back from finding the Lord by the way we act, so that no one can find fault with us and blame it on the Lord.

Chapter 7

2. Ethics

   1 Timothy 4:16 TLB

   Keep a close watch on all you do and think. Stay true to what is right and God will bless you and use you to help others.

3. Morality

   2 Timothy 2:22 TLB

   Run from anything that gives you the evil thoughts that young men often have, but stay close to anything that makes you want to do right...

4. Temperament

   2 Timothy 2:24,25 TLB

   God's people must not be quarrelsome; they must be gentle, patient teachers of those who are wrong.

5. Habits

   1 Timothy 4:8 TLB

   Bodily exercise is all right, but spiritual exercise is much more important and is a tonic for all you do. So exercise yourself spiritually and practice being a better Christian, because that will help you not only now in this life, but in the next life too.

6. Maturity

   1 Timothy 4:15 TLB

   Put these abilities to work; throw yourself into your tasks so that everyone may notice your improvement and progress.

II. Truthfulness

   A. Truth is not an option in life.

   Zechariah 8:16 TLB

   Here is your part: Tell the truth. Be fair. Live at peace with everyone.

B. Truth is the bedrock of integrity. Your personal integrity is the cornerstone of your character.

Psalm 24:4,5 TLB

Only those with pure hands and hearts, who do not practice dishonesty and lying.

They will receive God's own goodness as their blessing from him, planted in their lives by God himself, their Savior.

1. The more you base your life on truth, the better will be your way and the greater will be your life.

Proverbs 10:9

He that walketh uprightly walketh surely...

John 14:6

Jesus saith unto him, I am the way, the truth, and the life: no man cometh unto the Father, but by me.

2. The more you base your life on a lie, the harder will be your way, and the less significant will be your life.

Proverbs 13:15

...the way of transgressors is hard.

Proverbs 2:22 TLB

...evil men lose the good things they might have had, and they themselves shall be destroyed.

C. Truth is impartial.

James 3:17

But the wisdom that is from above is...without partiality...

D. Truth is eternal — it will stand firm.

Proverbs 12:19 TLB

Truth stands the test of time; lies are soon exposed.

Chapter 7

E. Truth eliminates guilt, fear and secrecy. Truth brings freedom.

John 8:32

And ye shall know the truth, and the truth shall make you free.

F. Men may know the truth, recognize truth, and even admit to truth, yet still fall for deception if they do not love the truth.

2 Thessalonians 2:10 TLB

He (the antichrist) **will completely fool those who...have said "no" to the Truth; (because) they have refused to believe it and love it, and let it save them.**

(Also **Titus 2:7**.)

G. If a person loves the truth, he will make it a part of his life.

James 1:21,22

...receive with meekness the engrafted word, which is able to save your souls.

But be ye doers of the word, and not hearers only, deceiving your own selves.

Titus 2:7 TLB

...Let everything you do reflect your love of the truth and the fact that you are in dead earnest about it.

III. Faithfulness

1 Corinthians 4:2

Moreover it is required in stewards, that a man be found faithful.

A. Faithfulness is the cornerstone of success.

Proverbs 28:20

A faithful man shall abound with blessings...

Matthew 24:46,47 TLB

"Blessings on you if I return and find you faithfully doing your work. I will put such faithful ones in charge of everything I own!"

B. God commits to character, not to talent.

Matthew 25:21

...Well done, thou good and faithful servant: thou hast been faithful over a few things, I will make thee ruler over many things: enter thou into the joy of thy lord.

Luke 16:10 TLB

"...For unless you are honest in small matters, you won't be in large ones. If you cheat even a little, you won't be honest with greater responsibilities."

(Also 2 Tim. 2:2.)

IV. Consistency

A. Inconsistency is a mark of immaturity.

Ephesians 4:14

That we henceforth be no more children, tossed to and fro, and carried about with every wind of doctrine...

B. Inconsistency takes a heavy toll on you and on those who depend upon you.

Proverbs 25:19 TLB

Putting confidence in an unreliable man is like chewing with a sore tooth, or trying to run on a broken foot.

C. Don't waste your youth by inconsistent thinking and behavior.

Ecclesiastes 12:1 TLB

Don't let the excitement of being young cause you to forget about your Creator. Honor him in your youth before the evil years come...

D. Instead, be committed to spiritual growth. Take the time necessary to develop holiness, wisdom and proficiency.

1 Timothy 4:7,8 TLB

... Spend your time and energy in the exercise of keeping spiritually fit. Bodily exercise is all right, but spiritual exercise is much more important and is a tonic for all you do. So exercise yourself spiritually and practice being a better Christian...

V. Openness

A. The mature person is willing to admit his wrong and to change.

Proverbs 28:13 TLB

A man who refuses to admit his mistakes can never be successful. But if he confesses and forsakes them, he gets another chance.

B. Spiritual maturity requires a willingness to leave behind old friendships and associations that would bind us to the world or our past life.

1 Corinthians 15:33 NIV

Do not be misled: "Bad company corrupts good character."

2 Corinthians 6:14 TLB

Don't be teamed with those who do not love the Lord, for what do the people of God have in common with the people of sin?...

VI. Individuality

A. To be true to God and yourself, you must find and fulfill His unique plan and purpose for your life.

Ephesians 2:10

For we are his workmanship, created in Christ Jesus unto good works, which God hath before ordained that we should walk in them.

B. You must not allow others to force you into their patterns of living. Learn from other people, but seek God to find the individual pattern He has for you alone.

Romans 12:2 Phillips

Don't let the world around you squeeze you into its own mould, but let God re-make you...

C. Do not allow yourself to partake of other men's sins, but follow after the Spirit of God.

1 Timothy 5:22

Lay hands suddenly on no man, neither be partaker of other men's sins: keep thyself pure.

1 Timothy 6:11

But thou, O man of God, flee these things; and follow after righteousness...

VII. Love

A. Love is the only motivation that is greater than the motivations of the world — fear, hate and greed.

1 John 4:18

There is no fear in love; but perfect love casteth out fear...

1 Peter 4:8 NIV

...love covers over a multitude of sins.

B. Most of what is called love today is really lust.

1 John 2:15,16 TLB

Stop loving this evil world and all that it offers you, for when you love these things you show that you do

not really love God; for all these worldly things, these evil desires — the craze for sex, the ambition to buy everything that appeals to you, and the pride that comes from wealth and importance — these are not from God. They are from this evil world itself.

C. The qualities of love are (1 Cor. 13:4-7 TLB):

Patience: ...Love is very patient...

Kindness: ...and kind...

Humility: ...never boastful or proud...

Generosity: ...never selfish...

Courtesy: ...or rude...

Unselfishness: ...does not demand its own way...

Temperance: ...is not irritable...

Guilelessness: ...rejoices whenever truth wins out...

Sincerity: ...will always believe in (the other person), ...always expect the best of him...

1. These qualities are the virtues of the real man. Manhood and Christlikeness are synonymous.

   Ephesians 4:15

   But speaking the truth in love, (we) may grow up into him in all things, which is the head, even Christ.

2. When the love of God is put in your heart by the Holy Ghost, these elements can be produced in your life.

   Romans 5:5

   ...the love of God is shed abroad in our hearts by the Holy Ghost which is given unto us.

D. God can command His children to love because love centers in the will, not the emotions.

   John 15:12 TLB

   "I demand that you love each other as much as I love you."

E. To be a man after God's own heart, turn your heart toward love. Rid yourself of every other motivation.

1 Timothy 1:5 TLB

What I am eager for is that all the Christians there will be filled with love that comes from pure hearts, and that their minds will be clean and their faith strong.

F. Allow the love of God to motivate you in your manhood just as it motivated Jesus when He walked the earth as the Son of man.

2 Corinthians 5:14,15 TLB

Whatever we do, it is certainly not for our own profit, but because Christ's love controls us now...He died for all so that all who live — having received eternal life from him — might live no longer for themselves, to please themselves, but to spend their lives pleasing Christ who died and rose again for them.

QUESTIONS TO CONSIDER:

1. List the ingredients of manhood.

2. Which do you believe is the primary ingredient? (See 1 Cor. 13.)

3. One definition of love is: "Seeking the highest good for others, even though they may be seeking the worst for you." How do you think having love would make it easier to acquire the other ingredients of manhood?

4. Why do you believe God can "command" His children to love? (See *Courage* pp. 112, 113.)

Read 1 John 4:10 and Romans 5:5. Where does our love for others originate?

Chapter 7

What should we do when we feel there is someone we just can't love?

Can our supply of love ever run out?

SCRIPTURE TO MEMORIZE:
Romans 8:29

Chapter 8 — BEND, BOW OR BURN

I. Dealing with loneliness

   A. Loneliness and being alone are two entirely different things.

      1. Being alone is sometimes necessary — even healthy, desirable, and appreciated. (Example: the Lord Jesus Christ.)

Matthew 14:23

And when he had sent the multitudes away, he went up into a mountain apart to pray: and when the evening was come, he was there alone.

      2. Loneliness is never desirable.

Psalm 142:4

I looked on my right hand, and beheld, but there was no man that would know me: refuge failed me; no man cared for my soul.

      3. The antidote to loneliness is friendship.

Proverbs 27:9

Ointment and perfume rejoice the heart: so doth the sweetness of a man's friend by hearty counsel.

      4. Friends are Heaven's riches.

Proverbs 17:17 TLB

A true friend is always loyal, and a brother is born to help in time of need.

   B. The desire to belong represents one of the most basic needs of man.

Genesis 2:18 TLB

And the Lord God said, "It isn't good for man to be alone..."

Chapter 8

1. Rejection is one of life's cruelest blows. (Example: the Lord Jesus Christ.)

   John 1:11

   He came unto his own, and his own received him not.

   Isaiah 53:3 TLB

   We despised him and rejected him — a man of sorrows, acquainted with bitterest grief. We turned our backs on him and looked the other way when he went by. He was despised and we didn't care.

2. A feeling of rejection is often the root cause of suicide. (Example: Elijah.)

   1 Kings 19:4,10 TLB

   Then he went on alone into the wilderness...and prayed that he might die...

   ..."I've got to die sometime, and it might as well be now...the people of Israel have...killed your prophets, and only I am left; and now they are trying to kill me, too."

II. Finding healing in the ministry of Jesus

   Psalm 34:18 TLB

   The Lord is close to those whose hearts are breaking; he rescues those who are humbly sorry for their sins.

   A. The ministry of the Lord Jesus to the human heart heals completely the trauma of loneliness, failure and rejection.

   Luke 4:18

   The Spirit of the Lord is upon me, because he hath anointed me to preach the gospel to the poor; he hath sent me to heal the brokenhearted, to preach deliverance to the captives, and recovering of sight to the blind, to set at liberty them that are bruised.

B. The Lord's healing, acceptance, power and grace gives the believer the ability to face the world and its reality.

Psalm 23:4,5

Yea, though I walk through the valley of the shadow of death, I will fear no evil: for thou art with me, thy rod and thy staff they comfort me.

Thou preparest a table before me in the presence of mine enemies: thou anointest my head with oil; my cup runneth over.

C. Jesus gives a peace, an inner stability, that is a mystery to the world but a comfort to the believer.

John 14:27

Peace I leave with you, my peace I give unto you: not as the world giveth, give I unto you. Let not your heart be troubled, neither let it be afraid.

(Also **Phil. 4:7.**)

1. In order to know the peace that passes all understanding, every area of life must be completely yielded to the Spirit of God.

    Romans 8:6 TLB

    Following after the Holy Spirit leads to life and peace, but following after the old nature leads to death.

2. Holding on to any sin will create confusion that will prevent the experiencing of God's peace.

    1 Peter 3:11,12 TLB

    Turn away from evil and do good. Try to live in peace even if you must run after it to catch and hold it!

    For the Lord is watching his children, listening to their prayers; but the Lord's face is hard against those who do evil.

Chapter 8

III. Resisting temptation

    A. Because of man's intense desire to be accepted and belong, there is always pressure upon him to go along with the gang.

    Proverbs 1:10,15 TLB

    If young toughs tell you, "Come and join us"...Don't do it, son! Stay far from men like that.

    B. The power of things yielded to in life grows stronger, while that which is resisted grows weaker.

    James 4:7

    Submit yourselves therefore to God. Resist the devil, and he will flee from you.

        1. When a person allows himself to be intimidated into doing what he knows to be wrong, he weakens his resolve to do right.

        Romans 6:16 TLB

        Don't you realize that you can choose your own master? You can choose sin (with death) or else obedience (with acquittal). The one to whom you offer yourself — he will take you and be your master and you will be his slave.

        2. The more an individual says "yes" to the things that are right, the stronger he becomes and the greater his ability to say "no" to wrong.

        Galatians 5:16

        This I say then, Walk in the Spirit, and ye shall not fulfil the lust of the flesh.

    C. This power to resist wrong is the key to success in life.

        1. When Jesus Christ faced temptation He overcame it with the Word of God.

Luke 4:4,8,12

And Jesus answered him, saying, It is written...

And Jesus answered and said unto him, Get thee behind me, Satan: for it is written...

And Jesus answering said unto him, It is said, Thou shalt not tempt the Lord thy God.

    2. His submission to the Father, resistance to the devil, and refusal to sin strengthened His spirit.

Luke 4:14 TLB

Then Jesus returned to Galilee, full of the Holy Spirit's power.

D. To succeed in life as Jesus did, rather than bending to the world's way, we Christians need to act in such a way as to influence people to conform to our godly standard of behavior.

Romans 12:2 TLB

Don't copy the behavior and customs of this world, but be a new and different person with a fresh newness in all you do and think. Then you will learn from your own experience how his (God's) ways will really satisfy you.

IV. Making the right choice

Deuteronomy 30:19

I call heaven and earth to record this day against you, that I have set before you life and death, blessing and cursing: therefore choose life, that both thou and thy seed may live.

    A. The freedom to choose between alternatives is the only true freedom in life.

Galatians 5:13

For, brethren, ye have been called unto liberty; only use not liberty for an occasion to the flesh, but by love serve one another.

Chapter 8

    B. As Christians, we can choose to succeed or to fail; we can be wise or ignorant.

       Psalm 90:12 TLB

       Teach us to number our days and recognize how few they are; help us to spend them as we should.

    C. Our choices are shown by the company we keep.

       Proverbs 27:19 TLB

       A mirror reflects a man's face, but what he is really like is shown by the kind of friends he chooses.

V. Avoiding the "church-wise"

    A. The church-wise are not those who genuinely love God and desire to seek and obey Him.

       Psalm 50:16,17 TLB

       ...Recite my laws no longer, and stop claiming my promises, for you have refused my discipline, disregarding my laws.

    B. The church-wise are men and women who have grown up in church, display all the proper cultural mannerisms, and mouth all the right religious words, yet do not have a vital living relationship with the Lord Jesus Christ.

       Isaiah 29:13

       Wherefore the Lord said,...this people draw near me with their mouth, and with their lips do honour me, but have removed their heart far from me, and their fear toward me is taught by the precept of men.

    C. Heaven is not reserved for the church-wise; it is the reward of the righteous.

       1. Only obedient spirits are allowed into Heaven.

Psalm 24:3,4

Who shall ascend into the hill of the Lord? or who shall stand in his holy place?

He that hath clean hands, and a pure heart...

2. Purity may not be popular in the world, but it is the rule of the day in Heaven.

Job 25:1 TLB

God is powerful and dreadful. He enforces peace in heaven.

3. God looks not at the outward facade of a person, but at the heart.

1 Samuel 16:7

...the Lord seeth not as man seeth; for man looketh on the outward appearance, but the Lord looketh on the heart.

(Also **1 Chron. 28:9.**)

D. To avoid falling into error, beware the church-wise.

Proverbs 13:20 TLB

Be with wise men and become wise. Be with evil men and become evil.

E. Remember: Sin is contagious, righteousness is not.

Haggai 2:11-14 TLB

Ask the priests this question about the law. "If one of you is carrying a holy sacrifice in his robes, and happens to brush against some bread or wine or meat, will it too become holy?"

"No," the priests replied. "Holiness does not pass to other things that way."

Then Haggai asked, "But if someone touches a dead person, and so becomes ceremonially impure, and then brushes against something, does it become contaminated?"

Chapter 8

And the priests answered, "Yes."

(Also 1 Cor. 15:33.)

F. Standing for righteousness may bring persecution, ridicule and rejection.

2 Timothy 3:12

Yea, and all that will live godly in Christ Jesus shall suffer persecution.

G. The fire you go through will purify and strengthen you.

1 Peter 1:7 TLB

These trials are only to test your faith, to see whether or not it is strong and pure. It is being tested as fire tests gold and purifies it — and your faith is far more precious to God than mere gold...

H. Don't waste your youth and manhood giving in to peer pressure from church-wise people.

Jeremiah 15:19,20 TLB

The Lord replied:..."You are to influence *them*, not let them influence *you!*

"They will fight against you like a besieging army against a high city wall. But they will not conquer you for I am with you to protect and deliver you, says the Lord."

VI. Building blocks of friendship

   A. Friendship is normal to life.

Ecclesiastes 4:9,10

Two are better than one... For if they fall, the one will lift up his fellow: but woe to him that is alone when he falleth; for he hath not another to help him up.

   B. Friendship must be cultivated.

Proverbs 18:24

A man that hath friends must shew himself friendly...

C. The common bond of friends is their trust.

Proverbs 17:17

A friend loveth at all times...

Proverbs 27:6

Faithful are the wounds of a friend...

D. If you find it difficult to find a friend you can trust, you can still become friends with God and ask Him to find other friends for you.

Psalm 16:2,3,5 TLB

I said to him (God), "You are my Lord; I have no other help but yours."

I want the company of godly men and women in the land; they are the true nobility...

The Lord himself is my inheritance, my prize.

E. Friendship with God is based on relationship, not religion.

Hosea 6:6 TLB

I don't want your sacrifices — I want your love; I don't want your offerings — I want you to know me.

1. How can God show Himself as a friend to us if we don't trust Him?

Nahum 1:7

The Lord is good, a strong hold in the day of trouble; and he knoweth them that trust in him.

2. How can God befriend us if He can't trust us?

Psalm 78:57 TLB

They (the rebellious children of Israel) **turned back from entering the Promised Land and disobeyed as** their fathers had. Like a crooked arrow, they missed the target of God's will...

3. If we give God our all, He will enable us to overcome anything that hinders us from being His friend.

1 Corinthians 10:13 TLB

...And no temptation is irresistible. You can trust God to keep the temptation from becoming so strong that you can't stand up against it, for he has promised this and will do what he says...

F. Resolve never to give up your life because of loneliness. Always remember that God is right there with you.

Hebrews 13:5,6 TLB

...For God has said, "I will never, never fail you nor forsake you." That is why we can say without any doubt or fear, "The Lord is my Helper and I am not afraid of anything that mere man can do to me."

QUESTIONS TO CONSIDER:

1. List several reasons why our choice of friends is so important to our lives.

2. ..."**Bad company corrupts good character**" (1 Cor. 15:33 NIV). Can you think of Biblical examples of people who made wrong choices because of the bad influence of companions? (Read 1 Kings 11:1-5; 12:1-14; Judges 16; 2 Chron. 24:1,2,15-25.)

Can you list the names of several people in the Bible who were strengthened and edified through good friendships? (Read. 1 Sam. 19,20; Acts 9:26,27; 11:25,26; 2 Tim. 1:1-3,16,17.)

Since friendships have such great potential for good or harm, do you believe we should get God's approval on our friendships?

3. Jesus was frequently criticized because of His choice of companions. The Bible tells us that man looks on the outward appearance but God looks at the heart. What do you suppose was the condition of heart of those who followed Jesus?

Of those who criticized Him?

SCRIPTURE TO MEMORIZE:

Hebrews 13:5,6

Chapter 9 — WRITE IT ON YOUR SHORTS

I. The importance of the written word

   A. Words are powerful. They are the only creative power man has.

   Proverbs 18:21

   Death and life are in the power of the tongue...

   B. There would be no Bible if men of God had not written down His revelation and truth.

   2 Peter 1:20,21 TLB

   For no prophecy recorded in Scripture was ever thought up by the prophet himself. It was the Holy Spirit within these godly men who gave them true messages from God.

   Romans 15:4 TLB

   These things that were written in the Scriptures so long ago are to teach us patience and to encourage us...

   C. The Lord speaks to His children through prayer and through His Word.

   Luke 24:32

   ...Did not our heart burn within us, while he talked with us by the way, and while he opened to us the scriptures?

   D. When David encountered his greatest crisis, he was able to strengthen himself by reviewing what God had done for him and his people in times past.

   1 Samuel 30:6

   And David was greatly distressed;...but David encouraged himself in the Lord his God.

E. To succeed in life, you need to pay careful attention to God's Word.

   1. Write down what God tells you.

     Proverbs 7:2,3 TLB

     ...Guard my words as your most precious possession. Write them down, and also keep them deep within your heart.

   2. Study every word God gives you.

     Job 23:12

     ...I have esteemed the words of his mouth more than my necessary food.

II. Qualities of success

  A. Decision

    1. Decision translates into energy.

      James 1:8

      A double minded man is unstable in all his ways.

    2. Decision motivates to action. (Example: Solomon.)

      2 Chronicles 2:1

      And Solomon determined to build an house for the name of the Lord...

    3. Write down your decision so you'll be motivated to hold to it.

      Habbakuk 2:2

      ...Write the vision, and make it plain upon tables, that he may run that readeth it.

  B. Dedication

    1. It takes dedication to reach your goal. (Example: Jesus.)

Luke 9:51 TLB

As the time drew near for his return to heaven, he moved steadily onward towards Jerusalem with an iron will.

2. Dedication and discipline enable you to overcome all obstacles.

Isaiah 50:7 TLB

Because the Lord helps me, I will not be dismayed; therefore, I have set my face like flint to do his will, and I know that I will triumph.

C. Details

1. Details make the difference between success and failure.

Joshua 11:15,16

As the Lord commanded Moses his servant, so did Moses command Joshua, and so did Joshua; he left nothing undone of all that the Lord commanded Moses.

So Joshua took all that land...

2. God is concerned with detail.

Matthew 10:29,30 TLB

Not one sparrow (What do they cost? Two for a penny?) can fall to the ground without your Father knowing it. And the very hairs of your head are all numbered.

Psalm 139:13,14 TLB

You made all the delicate, inner parts of my body, and knit them together in my mother's womb.

Thank you for making me so wonderfully complex! It is amazing to think about. Your workmanship is marvelous...

3. The first step in attending to details is to write them down. (Example: Commandments to the king.)

   Deuteronomy 17:18,19 TLB

   "And when he has been crowned and sits upon his throne as king, then he must copy these laws from the book kept by the Levite-priests. That copy of the laws shall be his constant companion."

D. Discipline

   1. All discipline is based on preference.

   1 Corinthians 9:25 TLB

   To win the contest you must deny yourselves many things that would keep you from doing your best. An athlete goes to all this trouble just to win a blue ribbon or a silver cup, but we do it for a heavenly reward that never disappears.

   2. Discipline is the correct application of pressure.

   1 Corinthians 9:27 TLB

   Like an athlete I punish my body, treating it roughly, training it to do what it should, not what it wants to...

   a. One of the tests of manhood is how a man handles pressure.

   Proverbs 24:10 TLB

   You are a poor specimen if you can't stand the pressure of adversity.

   b. Men must be tested and proven before they can be given authority.

   James 1:12 TLB

   Happy is the man who doesn't give in and do wrong when he is tempted, for afterwards he will get as his reward the crown of life that God has promised those who love him.

3. God draws lines for us and gives us boundaries for our lives so we won't be destroyed by sin.

Deuteronomy 30:19 TLB

"...I have set before you life or death, blessing or curse. Oh, that you would choose life; that you and your children might live!"

4. We must discipline ourselves in order to learn.

2 Timothy 2:15 TLB

Work hard so God can say to you, "Well done." Be a good workman, one who does not need to be ashamed when God examines your work. Know what His Word says and means.

III. Failure Factors

   A. Ignorance

   1. The core of ignorance is stubbornness.

   Hosea 4:6

   My people are destroyed for lack of knowledge: because thou hast rejected knowledge...

   2. Men fail because they have never learned how to learn.

   Proverbs 9:7-9 TLB

   If you rebuke a mocker, you will only get a smart retort,...he will only hate you for trying to help him...

   Teach a wise man, and he will be wiser; teach a good man, and he will learn more.

   Proverbs 10:8 TLB

   The wise man is glad to be instructed, but a self-sufficient fool falls flat on his face.

3. Men who read the Bible but don't apply it are spiritually ignorant.

   James 1:22-24 TLB

   And remember, it is a message to obey, not just to listen to. So don't fool yourselves.

   For if a person just listens and doesn't obey, he is like a man looking at his face in a mirror; as soon as he walks away, he can't see himself anymore or remember what he looks like.

4. Men repeat mistakes because they never learn from them.

   Proverbs 26:11 TLB

   As a dog returns to his vomit, so a fool repeats his folly.

B. Laziness

Proverbs 12:24 TLB
Work hard and become a leader; be lazy and never succeed.

1. Laziness is a sin.

   Romans 12:11 TLB

   Never be lazy in your work but serve the Lord enthusiastically.

2. Laziness brings poverty and destruction.

   Proverbs 10:4 TLB

   Lazy men are soon poor; hard workers get rich.

   Proverbs 18:9 TLB

   A lazy man is brother to the saboteur.

   Proverbs 13:4 TLB

   Lazy people want much but get little, while the diligent are prospering.

3. Procrastination is a form of laziness.

   Proverbs 12:11 TLB

   Hard work brings prosperity; only a fool idles away his time.

4. The man who talks most does least.

   Proverbs 14:23 TLB

   Work brings profit; talk brings poverty!

5. All a lazy man has to offer are excuses and opinions.

   Proverbs 26:13,16 TLB

   The lazy man won't go out to work. "There might be a lion outside!" he says...Yet in his own opinion he is smarter than seven wise men.

IV. Success qualities applied as principles

   A. *Decide* to be a man of God; write down your decision.

   Joshua 24:15

   ...but as for me and my house, we will serve the Lord.

   B. *Dedicate* yourself to studying and doing the Word (will) of God.

   Ezra 7:10

   For Ezra had prepared his heart to seek the law of the Lord, and to do it, and to teach in Israel statutes and judgments.

   C. *Detail* the will and plan of God for your life.

   1. Be a steward of God's words. Don't despise them by neglecting them.

   Isaiah 34:16 TLB

   Search the Book of the Lord and see all that he will do; not one detail will he miss;...for the Lord has said it, and his Spirit will make it all come true.

2. Write down everything He tells you.

Deuteronomy 6:6,9 TLB

"And you must think constantly about these commandments I am giving you today...write them on the doorposts of your house!"

3. Write down what God has taught you today and what He teaches you day by day in the future.

Revelation 1:19 TLB

Write down what you have just seen, and what will be shown to you.

D. *Discipline* yourself to do what God tells you to do.

1. Give God your immediate obedience.

Psalm 119:60

I made haste, and delayed not to keep thy commandments.

2. Remember that an ounce of obedience is worth a ton of prayer.

Psalm 40:6 TLB

It isn't sacrifices and offerings which you really want from your people...But you have accepted the offer of my life-long service.

(Also 1 Sam. 15:22.)

QUESTIONS TO CONSIDER:

1. What should we do when God speaks to us or teaches us something?

What does a careless attitude on our part toward the Word of God tell us about our desire to honor Him?

About our level of faith in Him?

About our willingness to obey Him?

2. What are four qualities needed for success with God and man?

Give some examples of how Jesus displayed each one of these qualities.

Do you believe the Lord can teach you how to develop these qualities in your own life?

Have you asked Him to help you do so?

SCRIPTURE TO MEMORIZE:

Psalm 119:11

Chapter 10 —
CHAMPIONS: MEN WHO NEVER QUIT

I. Champions are not those who never fail, they are those who never quit.

   A. Fear of failure is no reason for lack of commitment.

   2 Timothy 1:7

   For God hath not given us the spirit of fear; but of power, and of love, and of a sound mind.

   B. People love winners.

   1 Samuel 29:5 TLB

   "This is the same man the women of Israel sang about in their dances: 'Saul has slain his thousands and David his ten thousands!' "

   C. Champions are the right men, at the right place, at the right time.

   Ecclesiastes 3:1 TLB

   There is a right time for everything...

   D. To become a champion, you must see yourself as a champion.

   Philippians 4:13

   I can do all things through Christ which strengtheneth me.

II. Champions are made, not born.

   A. Champions are men in whom courage has become visible.

   1 Samuel 14:6 TLB

   "Yes, let's go across to those heathen," Jonathan had said to his bodyguard. "Perhaps the Lord will do a

miracle for us. For it makes no difference to him how many enemy troops there are!"

B. It is what a person does when he is alone that determines whether he will win or lose. (Example: Jesus.)

Luke 5:16 TLB

But he often withdrew to the wilderness for prayer.

C. If you want to be a champion in life, don't waste your youth.

Ecclesiastes 12:1 TLB

Don't let the excitement of being young cause you to forget about your Creator...

D. Remember: There is no gain without pain.

Hebrews 12:1,2 TLB

...and let us run with patience the particular race that God has set before us.

Keep your eyes on Jesus, our leader and instructor. He was willing to die a shameful death on the cross because of the joy he knew would be his afterwards...

1 Peter 4:1,2 TLB

Since Christ suffered and underwent pain, you must have the same attitude he did; you must be ready to suffer, too. For remember, when your body suffers, sin loses its power, and you won't be spending the rest of your life chasing after evil desires, but will be anxious to do the will of God.

III. There are four Hebrew root words for "man."

A. *ADAM:* Mankind, man in relationship to God (Gen. 1:26.)

B. *IYISH:* Male, husband, fellow, courageous (Gen. 2:24.)

CHAMPIONS: *Men Who Never Quit*

- C. *ENOWSH:* Mortal, weak, frailty, vulnerability (Ps. 103:15.)
- D. *GEBER:* Mature, valiant, hero, champion (Heb.: *el gibbor*, used in Isaiah 9:6 to refer to the expected Messiah and translated "mighty God") (Ps. 37:23.)

IV. Men who belong to God are to be members of a championship team.

- A. There are some vessels to honor, some to dishonor.

    2 Timothy 2:20,21 TLB

    In a wealthy home there are dishes made of gold and silver as well as some made from wood and clay. The expensive dishes are used for guests, and the cheap ones are used in the kitchen or to put garbage in.

    If you stay away from sin you will be like one of these dishes made of purest gold — the very best in the house — so that Christ himself can use you for his highest purposes.

- B. We are all members of the same team.

    Matthew 12:50 TLB

    ..."Anyone who obeys my Father in heaven is my brother, sister and mother!"

- C. We all train alone, but we all have in mind the same goal God has set for us personally to attain.

    Philippians 3:13,14 TLB

    No, dear brothers, I am still not all I should be but I am bringing all my energies to bear on this one thing: Forgetting the past and looking forward to what lies ahead, I strain to reach the end of the race and receive the prize for which God is calling us...

- D. Men who follow God are the right men, at the right place, at the right time.

Chapter 10

Psalm 37:23 TLB

The steps of good men are directed by the Lord. He delights in each step they take.

E. To be a true champion — a man of God — choose the more excellent way.

Psalm 16:11

Thou wilt shew me the path of life: in thy presence is fulness of joy; at thy right hand there are pleasures for evermore.

Be the man God wants you to be:
  A MAN OF GOD.
  A CHAMPION!

QUESTIONS TO CONSIDER:

1. "Champions are not those who never fail, they are those who never quit." Can you think of people in the Bible who refused to quit despite their failures and setbacks and who went on to become champions? (Read about Jacob in Gen. 27-35, Moses in Ex. 2-4, Joseph in Gen. 37,39-50, and Samson in Judges 16.)

Are there failures in your life which have discouraged you from joining God's championship team?

What should you do with those failures?

Have other people's opinions of you made you feel you could never be a champion?

What is God's opinion of you?

2. "Champions are the right men, in the right place, at the right time." In what ways does God help you meet these conditions? (See Ps. 37:23,24.)

3. Do you believe God wants you to be a champion?

As you read through *Courage* and this guide, which principles do you see that you need to add to your life in order to qualify for God's Championship Team?

What is God's part in bringing you success? (Read Phil. 1:6.)

SCRIPTURE TO MEMORIZE:

Philippians 1:6

References

American Standard Version (ASV). Copyright © 1901 by Thomas Nelson & Sons and copyright © 1929 by International Council of Religious Education. Thomas Nelson & Sons, Nashville, Tennessee.

The Amplified Bible, New Testament (AMP). Copyright © 1954, 1958 by The Lockman Foundation, La Habra, California.

The Holy Bible: New International Version (NIV). Copyright © 1973, 1978 by the International Bible Society. Used by permission of Zondervan Bible Publishers, Grand Rapids, Michigan.

The Living Bible (TLB). Copyright © 1971 by Tyndale House Publishers, Wheaton, Illinois.

The New Testament in Modern English (Phillips). Copyright © 1958, 1959, 1960, 1972 by J.B. Phillips. The Macmillian Publishing Co., Inc., New York, N.Y.

EDWIN LOUIS COLE
AUDIO TEACHING TAPES

AGREEMENT: THE PLACE OF POWER $20.00
(4 tapes)
    A study of the principle in Matthew 18:19. (A-102)

RELEASED $10.00
(2 tapes)
    Deals with deliverance, forgiveness, personal release from besetting sins, fear, and guilt. (A-107)

STRAIGHT TALK X-RATED $10.00
(2 tapes)
    Deals with one of the most common sins in the Church and the world today — sexual sin. (A-104)

MAXIMIZED MANHOOD SEMINAR $20.00
(4 tapes)
    Presents the life-changing principles of MAXIMIZED MANHOOD. Taped during a live satellite broadcast viewed by over 25,000 men. (A-109)

POTENTIAL PRINCIPLE SEMINAR $20.00
(4 tapes)
    Teaching on the plan God has for your success, based on the life of Joseph. Taped during a national satellite broadcast to over 800 churches. (A-114)

FOR WOMEN ONLY $20.00
(4 tapes)
A provocative series that will help women understand themselves and become the godly women the Lord has called them to be. (A-111)

FOR PARENTS ONLY $10.00
(2 tapes)
Draws lessons from the life of Eli, concerning the responsibility God places on the man in the home, and warns of the tragic consequences for the whole family when the father neglects his God-given authority. (A-112)

LEADERSHIP $30.00
(6 tapes)
The complete teaching from breath mints to Biblical exegesis. Start right, stay right with your church, Bible study group, or children's class. THIS IS A *MUST* FOR LEADERS!

Available from your local bookstore.

Video tapes are available.

For more information, or to receive Dr. Cole's publication, *COURAGE*, call Cole Ministries Headquarters at (817) 283-2898, or write:

EDWIN LOUIS COLE MINISTRIES
P. O. BOX 610588
Dallas, Texas 75261

BOOKS BY EDWIN LOUIS COLE

Maximized Manhood

Maximized Manhood Study Guide

The Potential Principle

*The Potential Principle
Scripture Reference Guide*

COURAGE
A Book For Champions

New from Harrison House

*The COURAGE
Scripture Reference Guide*

Available from your local bookstore.

A Division of Harrison House, Inc.
P. O. BOX 35035
TULSA, OK 74153

EDWIN LOUIS COLE

Internationally acclaimed speaker, television personality, best-selling author and motivational lecturer, known for his practical application of wisdom from kingdom principles.

Ed Cole has been called to speak with a prophetic voice to men, challenging them to fulfill their potential for true manhood, which is Christlikeness. He now travels extensively, exhorting young men to realize their dreams by disciplining themselves to God's favor, wisdom and courage.

NOTES